BACKYARD BIRD BOOK
for kids

by Janet Mohr with Adeline Howard

Devonshire Books

Appleton, WI, USA

BACKYARD BIRD BOOK FOR KIDS©

All rights reserved. No part of this book may be reproduced in any form whatsoever, by photography or xerography or by any other means, by broadcast or transmission, by translation into any kind of language, nor by recording electronically or otherwise, without permission in writing from the author, except by a reviewer, who may quote brief passages in critical articles or reviews.

First Edition 2010
Copyright 2010 by Janet Mohr
Devonshire Books, LLC.
918 W Browning St
Appleton, WI 54914
All rights reserved.
All photos by the author.
All photos were of live birds.
Printed in USA

ISBN   978-0-615-33660-2

Library of Congress Catalog Number: 2009941561

For children of all ages who love wildlife and the planet they live on.

With great appreciation to Scott Wilson, Jake Melampy, and Jim Beard for support and encouragement.

Hi! My name is Adeline. I am 8 years old. I have been watching birds in my Grandma's backyard for as long as I can remember. I thought it would be nice to have a book that had pictures of birds I see to easily tell which bird it is. So, here is that book. I hope it helps you when you watch birds in your backyard.

Before we start, I want to say a few things about bird watching. In order to get birds to come to your backyard there are a few things you need. Birds need food, water, a place to nest, and safe places to hide, like bushes.

You need food for the birds. If you have the food in bird feeders, you need to keep the feeders clean so the birds will stay healthy. Most feeders should be washed with germ-killing warm water and bleach or vinegar and soap at least once a month.

Hummingbird and oriole feeders need to be cleaned every 3-4 days. It's best to fill all feeders with only enough food for a short time and refill them often.

The birds also need water. A simple birdbath will work. If you have a pond, that works too. If the water sounds like it's moving, like a fountain, stream or waterfall, the birds will hear it and you will see more birds.

Birds also need shelter, a safe place to go to get away from animals that would eat them, like hawks and cats. A tree with big leaves or an evergreen is best.

Some birds will build nests in birdhouses. For these birds, you can make a birdhouse and put it up in your yard. We leave ours up in the winter so the birds can have a place to go during snowstorms and on very cold nights, but we clean them in the fall.

Now, let's move on to the birds. I have put pictures of birds in the book by color to help you find them more easily. Then, the first bird in a section will be smallest, and the last one will be the biggest. Not every bird will be in this book, but some of the most common birds are here. It's a good place to start.

Let's start with black or black and white birds. See the color tab on the side of the page? That will help you to easily find birds by their color.

This young **rose breasted grosbeak** is on his first migration, flying south for winter. His brown parts will soon turn black and his spotted front will turn white. The red spot on his chest will get deeper red. Grosbeaks eat seeds and will come to feeders. They usually nest in forested areas.

Downy and hairy woodpeckers look very much alike. The hairy woodpecker is much bigger than the downy and has a bigger bill. In both hairy and downy woodpeckers the adult males have a red spot on the top of their heads. Both will come to suet feeders and feeders with peanuts.

Downy

Hairy

The **common grackle** looks like it has a shiny, dark blue head in the sunlight. It is actually a blackbird. They make a call that sounds like, "Grack, grack, grack." It sort of sounds like they have a sore throat. They are smaller than crows, but bigger than robins.

You can't miss the **crow**! It is the largest blackbird you will see in your yard. It is all black, even its eyes, feet, and bill. In summer or winter, it is black. It makes a call that sounds like, "Caw, caw caw," which sounds like the bird is laughing. Crows eat just about anything, including small animals and seeds.

The **Eastern bluebird** likes to live in open, grassy fields. If you live near a field and you keep a mealworm feeder, you might see one. Their backs are sky blue and their fronts are a rusty red and white. They are larger than a sparrow, but smaller than a robin. Many people put up nesting boxes for them.

There are several types of **swallows**. They all eat flying bugs. Barn swallows live in barns and tree swallows, like this one, live near water. Tree swallows nest in boxes and fly out to swoop down and catch insects. They eat lots of bugs every day, so farmers like swallows. They are a little larger than a sparrow. If you get too near their nests they will swoop down at you. Barn swallows look like tree swallows except their front is orange, brighter than the Eastern bluebird.

The ***indigo bunting*** also likes wide open spaces and also eats bugs. They also eat seeds and might come to feeders. The males are a solid bright blue; the females are brown. This coloring helps the females hide from predators, like hawks, so they can raise chicks easier. They are about the size of a swallow, just a little bigger than a sparrow.

The **blue jay** is actually a blackbird, but it looks blue. The blue jay might be the first blue bird you see in your yard, and probably the only blue bird you see in winter. They are about the size of a grackle, and are very noisy. They make a loud screech to scare other birds away from feeders, so you will know when one is coming. They like corn and peanuts.

Hummingbirds, like these female ruby throated hummingbirds, are many people's favorite birds. These are the smallest of all birds, not much bigger than your parent's finger. They eat nectar from flowers and also eat bugs. Their bills are almost as long as their bodies. They flap their wings so fast that they make a humming sound. They also make a clicking sound. It is fun to watch them chase each other. They love bright red, tube-shaped flowers, and red nectar feeders. When the days get shorter, they fly south. Then you know summer is over.

The male **_goldfinch_** is one of the showiest birds in summer. He is bright yellow with black markings. Females are brownish green. They are about the size of a sparrow. They eat seeds, especially Nyjer (thistle) and black oil sunflower seed and really like mesh bag feeders. They turn light brown, like a dead leaf, in the fall. When they fly they sing a song that sounds like "life is good, life is good, life is good," and their flight pattern seems to match their song.

You might see **warblers** if you have the right kinds of plants, bushes and trees in your yard. They eat only bugs, so native plants that are not sprayed with bug killer are best. Many warblers have yellow on them and can sometimes be confused with female goldfinches. The warbler in this picture is a Tennessee warbler.

This **yellow warbler** is the most common warbler. This is also the brightest colored warbler. If you have lots of dense bushes near your house, you will be more likely to see warblers.

Male **house finches and purple finches** are very similar. Both are about the size of a sparrow. Both eat many kinds of seeds. Both have reddish coloring. The difference is purple finches are deeper red and house finches are more orange. Also, house finches have a streaked or spotted chest, and don't have a red crown.

House Finch

Purple Finch

Male **cardinals** are easy to spot, especially in winter. They are bright red with a black mask all year long. They are about the size of a robin. They love black oil sunflower and safflower seed. They start singing in January, the first sign that spring is coming. Their song sounds a little like a siren, "whoop, whoop, whoop, chirp-chirp-chirp." Because they do not fly south for the winter, their songs are a little different in different areas. They are sometimes pictured on holiday cards.

Male

Female

You might see a **redstart** if you have tall trees near your house. They are smaller than a robin or oriole. They also have less orange than an oriole, and their stomachs are white. They eat bugs and fruit. Their song is crisper and cleaner than the robin, although very similar.

Robins are one of the most common birds. Their orange chests makes them easy to identify. They eat worms, bugs and fruit. They are usually the first to arrive in spring and the last to leave in fall. The youngest robins may not fly south at all, but it is difficult for them to survive the winter in northern areas. If you have wintering robins, you might want to feed them raisins and moist dog food.

Northern orioles are one of the joys of spring. Their bright colors make them very popular with bird watchers. Males and females look similar except females are not as brightly colored. They build sack nests that hang from tall tree branches. They eat fruits, berries and orange nectar from feeders. If you put an orange half out for them they will come to it. They also like grape jelly. It is difficult to tell their song from the redstart's.

Male

Female

The **chipping sparrow** is a native sparrow and was not brought here from somewhere else. It flies south for the winter, but stays longer than bug eating birds. It is the smallest of the native sparrows and is named for the chipping sound it makes. Look for the bright rusty red-brown patch on its head. Like all native sparrows, it eats seeds, especially black oil sunflower, millet, and Nyjer seed. Like all true sparrows, males and females look the same.

This **house wren** is building a nest in a birdhouse. Wrens will nest in just about any cavity, or small covered hole they can find. If you have a wren nesting nearby, you will know it. The male sings almost constantly during nesting time. Wrens eat bugs, especially mosquitoes, and many people like them for this. They are just a little smaller than a sparrow. They come back early in spring and start singing. Can you see the difference in the shape of the bills in bug eating and seed eating birds?

Dark-eyed juncos come in this gray color and a more brown color, but they are the same bird. Both colors have a light colored chest and a darker back. They are smaller than a sparrow. They eat seeds, especially small seeds like millet (grass) and Nyjer (thistle). They migrate south to the US for winter and spend the summer in Canada. They arrive when all other birds are leaving.

Black-capped chickadees are one of the friendliest birds. If you have a little patience, you can get very close to them. They are about the same size as a junco, just a little smaller than a sparrow. Their song sounds like they are saying "chick-a-dee-dee-dee," which is where they got their name. They have another song that sounds like, "all clear, all clear." They eat seeds including black oil sunflower and smaller seeds. They also eat bugs and will come to suet feeders. They do not fly south for the winter.

English sparrows are probably one of the most common birds you will see. You might see them looking for scraps outside a restaurant or on city sidewalks. They will eat just about anything and live just about anywhere. They were brought here from England and are now taking food and nesting spots from other birds. Many people try to get rid of them because there are so many of them. They will attack other birds and steal their nests. They are actually a finch, not a sparrow.

Female

Male

Nuthatches do something other birds do not; they climb down trees headfirst looking for bugs. Most birds climb up trees. The red breasted and white breasted nuthatches look very similar except for their fronts. Also, the white breasted have strikingly bright heads, and are a bit larger than the red breasted nuthatch. They also eat seeds, especially peanuts and will come to suet feeders. Their song sounds slightly metallic, sort of like whi-whi-whi. They are a little smaller than sparrows.

Red Breasted Nuthatch

White Breasted Nuthatch

White crowned and white throated sparrows look very similar. The head of the white crowned sparrow looks much brighter than the white throated sparrow. But the white throated sparrow has a white patch under its bill and a yellow spot above its bill. Both are average sparrow size, a little bigger than a chipping sparrow. They usually nest in northern forests and come through on migration, eating seeds and fruits on the ground or in low bushes. If you put a little seed in a bare patch between bushes, you might see them.

White Throated Sparrow

White Crowned Sparrow

You might see a **phoebe** or a **thrush** if you have bushes near your yard. Phoebes and thrushes eat bugs, so thick bushes are best for them. You can tell phoebes by the sound they make, which sounds like phee-be, phee-be. Thrushes sound like the song of a flute. Phoebes and thrushes are almost the same size as a robin. If you see spots on the chest and it's brown, it's probably a thrush. If it's gray and clear chested, it's probably a phoebe.

Phoebe

Thrush

Cedar waxwings are one of the most elegant, sleek looking birds. They have red tips on their wings and yellow tips on their tails that look like they have been dipped in wax. That's where they get their name. They also look like they are wearing superhero masks. They eat fruit and bugs. If you have a crabapple or maple tree or berry bushes, you might see them. They are just a little smaller than a robin. They make a sound like a cricket and they travel in flocks, so if you hear crickets way up in a tree, look for cedar waxwings.

The **gray catbird** is a very smart bird. When another bird lays her eggs in a catbird nest, the catbird will move them out. Catbirds make a sound like a cat meowing. That is where they get their name. They eat bugs and fruit, and especially like wild grapes. They are a little smaller than a robin. They are very shy and you will probably hear them more than see them.

Mourning doves are very common. You almost get tired of seeing them. They eat seeds, and lots of them. They are just slightly larger than robins. They make a sound like coo, coo, coo that makes them seem very sad. That is why they are called mourning doves.

If you have bird feeders, you will probably also have **hawks**. This sharp-shinned hawk looks very similar to a Cooper's hawk. In fact, most people cannot tell the difference. Both eat small birds and sometimes small animals. They swoop over the roof of your house trying to surprise attack an unsuspecting bird at your feeder. When hawks are not successful and other birds know they are around, the neighborhood will get very noisy with birds sounding alarm calls. They are just a little bigger than a crow.

Mallards are common, and if you live near a pond, even a very small pond, you might see them. My Grandma's pond is not much bigger than a wading pool, but this pair visit it every year. They eat plants that grow in water like moss and algae. They are bigger than a crow. You can see them walking their chicks around many city parks and some neighborhoods.

Female

Male

There are many threats to birds in your backyard. House cats that prowl outside are a major threat to birds. (Being outside is also unsafe for the cat. Grandma's cat never goes outside, so this junco is not afraid.) Squirrels, chipmunks, and red squirrels are known to eat eggs and nesting chicks that cannot protect themselves.

Cat

Squirrel

I hope you have had fun learning a little more about the wildlife in your backyard. There are many other bird watching books that have many more birds and lots more information about the birds, but now you know the basics. Bird watching is a fun hobby that can last all your life!